macarons

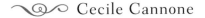 Cecile Cannone

macarons

Authentic French Cookie Recipes from the MACARON
CAFÉ

ULYSSES PRESS

Published by:
ULYSSES PRESS
PO Box 3440
Berkeley, CA 94703
www.ulyssespress.com

ISBN: 978-1-56975-820-5
Library of Congress Catalog Number 2010925862

Printed in Canada by Marquis Book Printing

10 9 8 7 6

Acquisitions editor: Kelly Reed
Managing editor: Claire Chun
Editor: Phyllis Elving
Proofreader: Lauren Harrison
Photography: HARA Partners, Inc.
Design and layout: what!design @ whatweb.com

To my mom and sisters, with whom I always had fun in the kitchen!

CONTENTS

❧ INTRODUCTION

Back in 1995, on a sunny afternoon in Central Park, my husband, Arnaud, and I were trying to figure out how to make our dream come true: We wanted to live in this amazing melting pot of Manhattan.

At that time our home was in Paris, where I had grown up. But in 2007, we returned to America from France with this oh-so-subtly-delicious recipe for a little almond delight called the *macaron*. We established our first MacarOn Café in New York's Fashion District, and French macarons—sometimes spelled "macaroons" (but pronounced ma-ka-RHON), not to be confused with the coconut cookies of the same name—quickly became the hot new treat in the neighborhood. We will never forget the fantastic welcome we received—the warmth and enthusiasm of the New Yorkers who flocked to our shop. Thanks to them, we even went beyond our original dream and opened a second location on Madison Avenue in the summer of 2010.

But the macaron phenomenon has exploded in popularity far beyond New York City.

Widely heralded as "the new cupcake," the macaron has been featured in media all over the country, and the craze shows

no sign of slowing down. And with the increasing market of consumers looking for gluten-free foods, macarons have become *the* trendy choice. They are made with almond flour, not wheat flour; sugar and egg whites are the other main ingredients.

Macarons come in innumerable flavors and hues but are brilliant in their simplicity: two delicate, crispy, soft shells, ready to be filled with jam, chocolate ganache, or buttercream. It is thought that they originated in Italy and were brought to France by Catherine de Medici in the sixteenth century. Their almond flavor and dome shape seduced the French court, and since then macarons have been served at the finest tables all over the world. Now it is your turn to make them and serve them at your own table!

With a little practice, and the guidance provided in the following pages, anyone can create these little delicacies at home. Offer them to your family, give them as gifts, or impress the guests at your next party. I will show you how you can personalize your macarons with sugar flowers or other decorations, and even how you can make macaron lollipops— perfect for children's birthday parties or baby showers. A tower

of macarons makes a dazzling centerpiece for your table, and has even been used as an alternative to a wedding cake. So use your imagination, and have fun.

A bientot!

Cecile Cannone
Owner and chef, MacarOn Café

***

✈ INGREDIENTS

Macaron shells call for only a short list of ingredients. For filling ingredients, see the recipes beginning on page 49.

Almond flour or almond meal

Check the date of packaging—you want the freshest almond flour possible. Store it in an airtight container in the bottom of your refrigerator. A day or two before baking, scoop up a handful of the almond flour and squeeze it between your fingers; if it sticks together, it will need to be dried out a bit. Spread it on a rimmed baking sheet and dry it in a 120°F oven for 10 minutes. If your oven temperature does not go that low, just use the lowest temperature available. Remove and let cool in a dry place. You can also grind your own almond flour using high-quality almonds.

Egg whites

Only the whites of the eggs are used for the macaron shells. Reserve the yolks for another recipe, such as Crème Brûlée (page 119). Separate whites from yolks 2 or 3 days before baking; store loosely covered in the refrigerator. Two hours before you start making your macarons, take the egg whites out of the refrigerator, uncover them, and let them come to room temperature.

Powdered egg whites

If you bake during especially humid weather, adding a small amount of powdered egg whites will help stabilize your macaron batter. You can buy powdered egg whites in many supermarkets, in specialty baking stores, or online.

Powdered sugar

Also called confectioners' or icing sugar, this has cornstarch added (usually about 3%) to prevent clumping; if you have a choice, the powdered sugar with the lowest percentage of cornstarch is best.

Granulated sugar

Choose superfine sugar (sometimes called ultrafine or baker's sugar) for your macaron shells—it's easily incorporated, producing a smooth batter and light texture.

Food coloring

You can color your macaron shells however you want—without coloring, they'll be pale brown. Gel paste food coloring is recommended over the liquid kind, since any excess moisture can cause the shells to crack.

ॐ EQUIPMENT

A convection oven (with a fan) is ideal for baking macarons—the heat circulates evenly throughout the oven, producing wonderful macarons with high "feet." A conventional electric oven can also be used; a gas oven is less successful for macarons. Every oven bakes differently, so be sure to use the correct temperature for the type of oven you have. The first time you bake macarons, carefully follow the timing and temperatures indicated in the recipe. Watch your macarons closely and adjust the baking time or temperature as necessary. For example, if your first batch starts to brown, bake the next tray for 1 minute less.

You'll need a precise scale, or dry measuring cups— quantities in this book are given in both volume (cups) and weight (ounces and grams); measuring your dry ingredients by weight will give you the most precise results.

liquid measuring cup

measuring spoons

electric mixer

food processor

strainer (medium size)

mixing bowls

rubber spatula

saucepan

candy thermometer (for Italian meringue macarons)

baking sheets

pastry bag

number-8 tip

parchment paper

timer

cooling racks

***

CHAPTER 1

The Shells

Macarons are made from two basic recipes for meringue:
French style and Italian style. The ingredients are the
same for both, but the amounts are a little different.
Try them both to see which one you like best.

The French version is especially sensitive to humidity, but the resulting cookie seems to melt in your mouth—exactly what we expect of a macaron. This is the recipe we use at the MacarOn Café.

The Italian macaron is more stable but has less of a "melting" quality. It's also a little more difficult to make, as you have to pour hot sugar syrup into your egg whites while beating them and you must be very precise with temperatures.

Since these little meringues are so sensitive to humidity, it's best to avoid baking when the weather is especially damp or humid (more than 60% relative humidity).

Before you bake

To make a template for piping your macaron shells, draw 2½-inch circles on a large sheet of paper, using a compass or tracing around a cookie cutter or a small glass. Space the circles 1 inch apart. Position this pattern on your baking sheet, then place parchment paper on top of it. After piping your shells, carefully pull out the pattern to use on the next baking sheet.

French meringue macarons

Makes 50 to 60 shells, for 25 to 30 filled macarons

2¾ cups (8.8 ounces/250 grams) almond flour

2¾ cups (12.4 ounces/350 grams)
powdered sugar

1 cup egg whites (from 7 or 8 eggs),
at room temperature

pinch of salt

2 teaspoons powdered egg whites,
if weather is humid

¾ cup (5.3 ounces/150 grams) superfine
granulated sugar

5 to 7 drops gel paste food coloring
(optional)

STEP 1: Line your baking sheets with parchment paper.

STEP 2: Blend the almond flour with the powdered sugar in the food processor to make a fine powder (or sift together, discarding any large crumbs and adding a bit more almond flour and powdered sugar as needed to compensate). Then sift the mixture through a strainer until it's as fine as you can get it. This keeps crumbs from forming on the macaron tops as they bake.

STEP 3: With the wire whip attachment on the electric mixer, beat the egg whites with the salt and the powdered egg whites (if you're using them), starting slowly and then increasing speed as the whites start to rise. Add the granulated sugar and the food coloring. Beat until the egg whites form stiff peaks and your meringue is firm and shiny.

STEP 4: Pour the beaten egg whites onto your almond flour mixture and gently fold them in, using a rubber spatula. Move your spatula from the bottom of the bowl to the edges with one hand, using your other hand to rotate the bowl. Now hit the spatula against the rim of the bowl until the batter falls in a wide ribbon when you raise the spatula. When you can't see any crumbs of almond flour and the mixture is shiny and flowing, you're ready to start piping.

The French have a special word—*macaronner*—to describe the physical action of mixing all the ingredients for macarons. This has to be done by hand. You cannot do it with your mixer—you must be able to feel the consistency of the macaron batter.

STEP 5: Fit your pastry bag with a number-8 tip and fill with batter. Start by squeezing out a small amount of mix onto a parchment-lined baking sheet to form a 2½-inch circle. Be sure to leave 1 inch of space between macarons so they will not touch each other while they bake.

If the peak that forms on the top of the macaron does not disappear after piping, it means the batter could have been beaten a little more. To eliminate the peaks, tap the baking sheet on the tabletop, making sure to hold the parchment paper in place with your thumbs.

Let the piped macarons rest for 15 minutes. Preheat the oven to 300°F (325°F for a non-convection oven).

Using a pastry bag requires some practice. It may seem awkward at first, but you'll soon get the hang of it.

Prepare the bag (if it hasn't been used before) by cutting about 2 inches off the narrow end—just enough so that when you insert a number-8 decorating tip, about a third of the tip extends outside the bag. Push the tip firmly in place and spoon in your filling, leaving enough room at the top to twist the bag shut. It's best to fill the bag with half of the batter at a time so it's not too heavy. To make it easier to fill your pastry bag, place it upright in an empty jar or other straight-sided container. This will help steady the bag while you fill it with batter.

Squeezing the bag slowly, pipe each macaron shell out in a single dollop. Lift the bag quickly to finish.

STEP 6: Bake for 14 minutes. After the first 5 minutes, open the oven door briefly to let the steam out.

Let the macarons cool completely on a rack before taking them off the parchment paper. Press the bottom of a cooled baked macaron shell with your finger; it should be soft. If the bottom of the shell is hard, reduce the baking time for the rest of your macarons from 14 minutes to 13 minutes.

✳✳✳

Italian meringue macarons

Makes 60 shells, for 30 filled macarons

1 cup egg whites
(from 7 or 8 eggs), at room temperature

3 cups (10.6 ounces/300 grams)
almond flour

2¼ cups (10.6 ounces/300 grams)
powdered sugar

2 teaspoons powdered egg whites,
if weather is humid

6 tablespoons water

1½ cups (10.6 ounces/300 grams) superfine
granulated sugar

pinch of salt

5 to 7 drops gel paste food coloring
(optional)

STEP 1: Line your baking sheets with parchment paper. Divide the egg whites equally into two bowls.

STEP 2: Blend the almond flour with the powdered sugar in your food processor to make a fine powder (or sift together, discarding large crumbs and adding a little more almond flour and powdered sugar as

needed to compensate). Then sift the mixture through a strainer until it's as fine as you can get it. This keeps crumbs from forming on the macaron tops as they bake.

STEP 3: Add the powdered egg whites if you are using them. Now slowly stir in one bowl of the egg whites. Set aside.

STEP 4: In a saucepan, start heating the water and the granulated sugar to 245°F (use a candy thermometer to monitor the temperature). In the meantime, begin beating the remainder of the egg whites and the salt with the wire whip attachment on the electric mixer, keeping an eye on your saucepan and thermometer as the egg whites rise.

STEP 5: Watch the thermometer in the hot sugar syrup carefully. When the hot sugar syrup is at the desired temperature, pour it slowly into the egg whites along the edge of the bowl and turn up the mixer speed. Add food coloring if you're using it. Continue beating until the egg whites form stiff peaks and the mixture has cooled down. Fold the beaten whites into the almond flour mixture, as described in Step 4 on page 31. You want your batter to be shiny and flowing, but not liquid.

STEP 6: Using a pastry bag with a number-8 tip, pipe your macarons in 2½-inch circles onto parchment-lined baking sheets. Be sure to leave 1 inch of space between them.

If the peak that forms on the top of the macaron does not disappear after piping, it means the batter could have been beaten a little more. To eliminate the peaks, tap the baking sheet on the tabletop, making sure to hold the parchment paper in place with your thumbs.

Let the piped macarons rest for 15 minutes. Preheat the oven to 300°F (325°F for a non-convection oven).

STEP 7: Bake for 14 minutes. After the first 5 minutes, open the oven door briefly to let the steam out.

Let the macarons cool completely on a rack before taking them off the parchment paper.

✃ PROBLEMS AND SOLUTIONS

Most of the difficulties that can arise when you make macarons have to do with humidity and temperature. Here are some recommendations for eliminating any "shell problems."

Cracks in the shells

- If you're baking Italian meringue macarons, it's very important to keep a close watch on both the egg whites in the mixer and the sugar syrup on the stove. If you pour your hot sugar syrup before the egg whites are stiff enough, the macarons will crack when they bake.

- Bake only one sheet at a time to avoid creating too much humidity in the oven.

- Don't pipe too many macarons onto a baking sheet—it will create too much humidity in the oven. Leave an inch of space between macarons; a half sheet pan (18 by 13 inches) will hold 20 shells.

- Using a decorating tip that is too small will create moisture when the batter is piped out of the pastry bag. A number-8 tip is perfect.

- If it seems especially humid in your kitchen (60% relative humidity or more), double the amount of powdered egg whites in your batter and increase the baking time by 1 or 2 minutes.

- Letting the egg whites sit at room temperature longer before baking will help moisture to evaporate.

- Rest your piped macarons for a full 15 minutes before you bake them. If the first batch cracks, double the resting time for the remaining macarons.

Lumps on the shells

- Be sure your almond flour and powdered sugar mixture is as fine as you can sift it (Step 2). If you still have crumbs on the baked shells, try a finer strainer.

Stains on the shells

- Stains usually appear when the batter has been mixed too much. Avoid excessive mixing on your next try. It's better for batter to be under-mixed than over-mixed. While under-mixed batter may result in peaks on your piped macarons, these are easily fixed by tapping the bottom of the baking sheet on the tabletop after you've piped your macarons. Stains caused by over-mixing, however, can't be remedied.

Air bubbles

- If your macarons aren't solid all the way through and you see air bubbles in the shells, you're incorporating too much air in the batter. When you mix all the ingredients together—the *macaronner* process—slap the sides of the bowl more times to take air out of the batter.

- Let the piped macarons rest longer before baking (30 minutes instead of 15 minutes).

Sticky feet on the parchment paper

- Let the macarons cool completely before peeling them off the parchment paper. If they still stick, try increasing the baking time by 2 to 4 minutes. Fluxuating oven temperature can result in under-baking.

No feet at all

- No rest = no feet. Let your piped macarons rest at least 15 to 30 minutes before you put them in the oven so they will have nice "feet" that you can see rising during the first minute of baking.

CHAPTER 2
Fillings

Now it's time to fill your macaron shells. Here we present some of the most classic recipes for fillings, from chocolate ganache to flavored buttercreams to homemade jams. Be sure to plan ahead—some fillings must "set" before they're ready to use.

Assembling your macarons is simple. Arrange the bottom shells flat side up on a tray, then place about a teaspoonful of filling in the center of each, using a spoon or a pastry bag (depending on the type of filling). Then twist on the top shells, flat side down, to form the macaron "sandwiches."

Different kinds of fillings call for different resting times to allow the flavors to develop in the shells. Follow the instructions for the specific filling types.

✳✳✳

CHOCOLATE GANACHE

Let's start with dark chocolate ganache—always our bestseller! Whichever ganache variation you use, let your filled macarons rest for 12 hours in the refrigerator before serving them so that the aroma of the filling can develop into the shells.

To assemble the macarons, fit a pastry bag with a number-8 tip, spoon in your ganache, and pipe it onto the bottom shells. (Alternately, you can spread it on with a teaspoon, but a pastry bag gives a more uniform, professional effect.) Twist on the tops, cover airtight with plastic wrap, and refrigerate.

Each of the following recipes makes enough filling for one recipe of shells (25 to 30 filled macarons). Refrigerate any leftover ganache, but let it come to room temperature before using it as a filling.

Dark chocolate ganache

7 ounces (200 grams) dark chocolate (65% to 70% cocoa content), cut in little pieces, OR dark chocolate chips

1⅓ cups heavy cream

1 tablespoon honey

2 tablespoons (1 ounce/28 grams) unsalted butter, preferably European-style

In a saucepan over low heat, gently stir together the chocolate, heavy cream, and honey until the chocolate is melted and the ingredients are perfectly blended. Remove from heat, let cool for a few minutes, and stir in the butter.

Pour into a bowl and let cool for 30 minutes at room temperature, until thick enough to spread or pipe.

Fit a pastry bag with a number-8 tip, fill with ganache, and pipe onto the macaron bottoms, or spread on with a teaspoon. Twist on the tops, cover airtight with plastic wrap, and refrigerate the filled macarons for 12 hours to let the aroma of the filling develop into the shells.

Dark chocolate–coconut ganache

6 ounces (170 grams) dark chocolate (65% to 70% cocoa content), cut in little pieces, OR dark chocolate chips

1¼ cups heavy cream

½ teaspoon vanilla extract
OR the seeds from 1 vanilla bean

1½ cups (4 ounces/124 grams) shredded coconut flakes, as fine as possible

In a saucepan over low heat, gently stir together the chocolate, heavy cream, and vanilla until the chocolate is melted and perfectly blended in. Mix in the coconut. Pour into a bowl and let cool for 30 minutes at room temperature, until thick enough to spread or pipe.

Chocolate-orange ganache

7 ounces (200 grams) dark chocolate (65% to 70% cocoa content), cut in little pieces, OR dark chocolate chips

1⅓ cups heavy cream

5 teaspoons candied orange peel cut in very small pieces OR 1 teaspoon orange extract plus the grated zest of one orange

2 tablespoons (1 ounce/28 grams) unsalted butter, preferably European-style

In a saucepan over low heat, gently stir together the chocolate and the heavy cream until the chocolate is melted and perfectly blended in. Let cool a few minutes and stir in the orange peel, or orange extract and zest, and the butter. Pour into a bowl and let cool for 30 minutes at room temperature before piping.

White chocolate ganache

7 ounces (200 grams) white chocolate, cut in little pieces, OR white chocolate chips

1 cup heavy cream

1 tablespoon honey

3½ tablespoons (1.7 ounces/50 grams) unsalted butter, preferably European-style

In a saucepan over low heat, gently stir together the white chocolate, heavy cream, and honey until the chocolate is melted and perfectly blended in. Pour into a bowl and let cool to room temperature; or put it in the refrigerator for 5 minutes to cool more quickly, checking to make sure the chocolate doesn't get too hard.

When the ganache is completely cool, transfer it to your mixer bowl and begin beating at high speed using the paddle accessory or wire whip attachment. Add the butter in small pieces and let it work in until you have a light and fluffy white chocolate cream.

Chocolate-ginger ganache

For decoration, place a little piece of ginger on half of the shells (the macaron tops) before you bake them.

7 ounces (200 grams) dark chocolate (65% to 70% cocoa content), cut in little pieces, OR dark chocolate chips

1¼ cups (10 fluid ounces) heavy cream

2 tablespoons (20 grams) candied ginger, cut in very small pieces with scissors

2 tablespoons (1 ounce/28 grams) unsalted butter, preferably European-style

In a saucepan over low heat, gently mix the chocolate with the heavy cream until the chocolate is melted and perfectly blended in. Let cool a few minutes and then stir in the candied ginger and the butter. Pour into a bowl and let cool for 30 minutes at room temperature before piping.

Chocolate–passion fruit ganache

7 ounces (200 grams) dark chocolate (65% to 70% cocoa content), cut in little pieces, OR dark chocolate chips

½ cup (3.5 ounces/100 grams) frozen passion fruit puree or juice

2 tablespoons (1 ounce/28 grams) chilled unsalted butter, preferably European-style

Melt the chocolate in the microwave oven, or in the top of a double boiler over simmering water on the stovetop. Heat the passion fruit puree or juice in the microwave or on the stovetop. If using a stovetop, remove the pans from the heat, then slowly add the passion fruit to the chocolate and mix well. Add the butter, stirring until the ingredients are perfectly blended. Pour into a bowl and let cool for 30 minutes at room temperature, until thick enough to spread or pipe.

Chocolate–peanut butter ganache

1 recipe Dark chocolate ganache (page 54)
1 (16-ounce) jar creamy peanut butter

Fill one pastry bag with the dark chocolate ganache and another with the peanut butter. Pipe chocolate ganache onto half of each macaron bottom, then pipe peanut butter onto the other half. Twist on the macaron tops.

BUTTERCREAM

Buttercream is a popular macaron filling that can be made in endless flavor variations. Always use high-quality real butter, never margarine or substitutes. Feel free to put your own twist on the following recipes. You love vanilla with chocolate? Add a half cup of chocolate chips to your vanilla buttercream.

Be sure that your buttercream is perfectly mixed (no visible crumbs of butter, please!), and then spoon it into a pastry bag to pipe onto the macaron bottoms, using a number-8 tip; or spread it on with a spoon. (A pastry bag creates a more uniform finish.) Your filled macarons will be best if they are refrigerated, wrapped airtight, for several hours or overnight—provided you can wait that long!

Each of the following recipes makes enough filling for one recipe of macaron shells (25 to 30 filled macarons). Any leftover buttercream will keep in the refrigerator for 4 or 5 days, to be used for more macarons or as a filling for a cake.

Pistachio buttercream

Dress up your filled macarons by rolling the edges in finely ground pistachios spread on a plate or in a small bowl.

3 eggs

1 cup (7 ounces/200 grams) superfine granulated sugar

½ cup (1.8 ounces/50 grams) ground raw pistachios OR 2 tablespoons (1 ounce/30 grams) canned pistachio paste

1 cup plus 2 tablespoons (2¼ sticks; 9 ounces/230 grams) chilled unsalted butter, preferably European-style

Beat together the eggs and the sugar with the electric mixer at high speed; you want your batter to double in volume and become fluffy. Pour into a saucepan, then stir in the pistachios. Heat over medium temperature, stirring, until the mixture forms a compact batter. Pour into a shallow dish, cover with plastic wrap, and chill in the refrigerator.

Cut the butter into small pieces and beat with the mixer at high speed, using the wire whip attachment. When the butter starts to expand in volume and become fluffy, add the chilled pistachio batter and whip again.

Vanilla buttercream

3 eggs

1 cup (7 ounces/200 grams) superfine granulated sugar

1 tablespoon vanilla extract or vanilla paste OR the seeds from 2 vanilla beans

1 cup plus 2 tablespoons (2¼ sticks; 9 ounces/230 grams) chilled unsalted butter, preferably European-style

Beat together the eggs and the sugar with the electric mixer at high speed; you want your batter to double in volume and become fluffy. Pour into a saucepan, add the vanilla, and heat over medium temperature, stirring, until it forms a compact batter. Pour into a shallow dish, cover with plastic film, and chill in the refrigerator.

Cut the cold butter into small pieces and beat with the electric mixer at high speed, using the wire whip attachment. When the butter starts to expand in volume and become fluffy, add the cold vanilla batter and whip again.

Rose buttercream

3 eggs

1 cup (7 ounces/200 grams) superfine granulated sugar

1 cup rose water (can be purchased in many specialty grocery stores or online)

1 cup plus 2 tablespoons (2¼ sticks; 9 ounces/230 grams) chilled unsalted butter, preferably European-style

5 to 8 drops edible essential rose oil (optional) to enhance the taste of the buttercream

Beat together the eggs and the sugar with the electric mixer at high speed. You want your batter to double in volume and become fluffy. Pour into a saucepan over medium heat, add the rose water, and stir until the liquid evaporates and the mixture forms a compact batter. Pour into a shallow dish, cover with plastic wrap, and chill in the refrigerator.

Cut the cold butter into small pieces and beat at high speed, using the mixer's wire whip attachment. When the butter starts to expand in volume and become fluffy, add the chilled rose batter and whip again. For a stronger rose flavor, add a few drops of the rose oil; how much you need depends on the brand.

***

Pistachio & rose buttercream

1 recipe Pistachio buttercream (page 71)
1 recipe Rose buttercream (page 74)

Fill one pastry bag with the pistachio buttercream, another with the rose buttercream. Pipe pistachio buttercream onto one half of each macaron bottom, then pipe the rose buttercream onto the other half. Twist on the tops.

Lemon buttercream

3 eggs

1 cup (7 ounces/200 grams) superfine granulated sugar

grated zest from 2 large lemons

½ cup lemon juice (about 2 large lemons)

1 cup plus 2 tablespoons (2¼ sticks; 9 ounces/230 grams) chilled unsalted butter, preferably European-style

Beat together the eggs and the sugar with the electric mixer at high speed. You want your batter to double in volume and become fluffy. Pour into a saucepan over medium heat, add the lemon zest and juice, and stir until the liquid evaporates and the mixture forms a compact batter. Pour into a shallow dish, cover with plastic wrap, and chill in the refrigerator.

Cut the cold butter into small pieces and beat at high speed, using the mixer's wire whip attachment. When the butter starts to expand in volume and become fluffy, add the chilled lemon batter and whip again.

Lavender buttercream

3 eggs

1 cup (7 ounces/200 grams) superfine granulated sugar

1 cup lavender water (directions on page 82)

1 cup plus 2 tablespoons (2¼ sticks; 9 ounces/230 grams) chilled unsalted butter, preferably European-style

5 to 8 drops edible essential lavender oil (optional)

Beat together the eggs and the sugar with the electric mixer at high speed; you want your batter to double in volume and become fluffy. Pour into a saucepan, add the lavender water, and heat at medium temperature, stirring, until the liquid evaporates and the mixture forms a compact batter. Pour into a shallow dish, cover with plastic wrap, and chill in the refrigerator.

Cut the cold butter into small pieces and beat at a high speed with the mixer's wire whip attachment. When the butter starts to increase in volume and become fluffy, add the cold lavender batter and whip again. For a stronger lavender flavor, add a few drops of edible essential lavender oil; how much you need depends on the brand.

Lavender water: Rinse several fresh lavender stems and pour boiling water over them in a bowl; steep for 5 minutes. Strain.

✳✳✳

Chestnut buttercream

*For the crushed chestnuts in this recipe, you can use canned or
frozen chestnuts. If you can't find any, simply omit this ingredient.
Any leftover filling can be kept in the refrigerator for 2 or 3 days.
Use it to fill a layer cake, or cupcakes split in half.*

1 cup (9 ounces/250 grams) chestnut
puree

4 to 6 tablespoons (1.8 ounces/50 grams)
crushed, cooked chestnuts

1 tablespoon whiskey OR 1 teaspoon vanilla
extract (depending on taste preference)

1 cup plus 2 tablespoons (2¼ sticks;
9 ounces/230 grams) chilled unsalted
butter, preferably European-style

With the electric mixer at high speed, beat together the chestnut puree,
crushed chestnuts, and whiskey or vanilla. Gradually add the butter, cut
in small pieces, and beat until it's perfectly blended in.

Apple-cinnamon buttercream

3 eggs

1 cup (7 ounces/200 grams) superfine granulated sugar

1 cup applesauce

1 apple, cored and chopped (including peel)

1 tablespoon cinnamon

1 cup plus 2 tablespoons (2¼ sticks; 9 ounces/230 grams) chilled unsalted butter, preferably European-style

Beat together the eggs and the sugar with the electric mixer at high speed; you want your batter to double in volume and become fluffy. Pour into a saucepan, stir in the applesauce and the chopped apple, and heat at medium temperature, stirring continuously until the mixture forms a compact batter. Pour into a shallow dish, cover with plastic wrap, and chill in the refrigerator.

When the batter is cold, add the cinnamon and the butter, cut in small pieces; beat at high speed, using the mixer's wire whip attachment, until no butter pieces are visible.

Pumpkin-cinnamon buttercream

3 eggs

1 cup (7 ounces/200 grams) superfine granulated sugar

2 cups canned pumpkin pie mix

1½ tablespoons cinnamon

1 cup plus 2 tablespoons (2¼ sticks; 9 ounces/230 grams) chilled unsalted butter, preferably European-style

Beat together the eggs and the sugar with the electric mixer at high speed; you want your batter to double in volume and become fluffy. Pour into a saucepan, add the pumpkin mix and cinnamon, and heat at medium temperature, stirring continuously until the mixture forms a compact batter. Pour into a shallow dish, cover with plastic wrap, and chill in the refrigerator.

When the batter is cold, add cold butter, cut in small pieces; beat at high speed, using the mixer's wire whip attachment, until no butter pieces are visible.

Gingerbread buttercream

3 eggs

1 cup (7 ounces/200 grams) superfine granulated sugar

1 tablespoon gingerbread spice blend

1 cup plus 2 tablespoons (2¼ sticks; 9 ounces/230 grams) chilled unsalted butter, preferably European-style

Beat together the eggs and the sugar with the electric mixer at high speed. You want your batter to double in volume and become fluffy. Pour into a saucepan over medium heat, add the gingerbread spice, and stir until the mixture forms a compact batter. Pour into a shallow dish, cover with plastic wrap, and chill in the refrigerator.

Cut the cold butter into small pieces and beat at high speed, using the mixer's wire whip attachment. When the butter starts to expand in volume and become fluffy, add the chilled gingerbread batter and whip again. For a stronger gingerbread flavor, add more gingerbread spice and mix again.

Espresso buttercream

3 eggs

1 cup (7 ounces/200 grams) superfine granulated sugar

1 tablespoon instant espresso grounds (or 2 tablespoons prepared espresso)

1 cup plus 2 tablespoons (2¼ sticks; 9 ounces/230 grams) chilled unsalted butter, preferably European-style

Beat together the eggs and the sugar with the electric mixer at high speed. You want your batter to double in volume and become fluffy. Pour into a saucepan over medium heat, add the espresso, and stir until the mixture forms a compact batter. Pour into a shallow dish, cover with plastic wrap, and chill in the refrigerator.

Cut the cold butter into small pieces and beat at high speed, using the mixer's wire whip attachment. When the butter starts to expand in volume and become fluffy, add the chilled espresso batter and whip again.

HOMEMADE JAM

Jams make great fillings for macarons. Using either fresh or frozen fruit, it's easy to make them yourself. Prepare your jam at least a day ahead—jams need to congeal before you use them as fillings.

This recipe works with most kinds of fruit. Be creative! Combine a variety of berries, mix rhubarb and strawberries, flavor pear jam with vanilla, or add almond slices to apricot jam.

STORING YOUR MACARONS

Once your macarons are filled, here's how to store them so they won't lose their delicious taste and texture.

Remember—macarons are extremely sensitive to moisture in the air. The best way to keep your macarons safe from humidity is to store them in airtight plastic containers in the refrigerator. They will keep this way for up to 7 days. For longer storage, you can freeze macarons for as long as 6 months.

Allow macarons to come to room temperature before serving them; if they are frozen, take them out of the freezer 3 hours ahead of time. Any macarons that aren't eaten should go back into the refrigerator.

2¼ pounds (1 kilogram) fresh or frozen fruit (raspberries, apricots, or rhubarb, for example)

4¾ cups (2 pounds/900 grams) granulated sugar

1 teaspoon dry pectin, or as package directs

Rinse fresh fruit, remove pits, and cut into pieces, as needed; frozen fruit is ready to use as packaged.

In a large saucepan over low heat, mix the fruit with the sugar and the pectin; stir gently. Gradually increase the burner temperature. As soon as the mixture starts bubbling (around 200°F), set a timer for 5 minutes and begin stirring in large circular motions, always in the same direction. After 5 minutes, turn off the heat and let the jam cool in the pan for 15 minutes before pouring it into glass jars or other containers.

Refrigerate your jam for a day. To use as a filling, place a teaspoonful in the center of a macaron shell, then twist another shell in place on top. Cover the filled macarons airtight with plastic wrap and let them rest for 24 hours in the refrigerator. Jams contain more liquid than chocolate ganache does, so the macarons need more resting time in order for the filling to set.

Leftover jam can be kept in the refrigerator for a week. Enjoy it on your breakfast toast or muffins, or use it to fill a layer cake.

*** ***

MORE FILLING IDEAS

In addition to making your own macaron fillings, you can get creative with other classic flavors to fill your shells:

Nutella

Dulce de leche (toffee caramel)

Peanut butter

Peanut butter & jam

Lemon curd

Or use a combination of recipes from this book for even more possibilities.

Mocha

1 recipe Espresso buttercream (page 93)
1 recipe Dark chocolate ganache (page 54)

Fill one pastry bag with the espresso buttercream, and another with the dark chocolate ganache. Pipe espresso buttercream onto half of each macaron bottom, then pipe dark chocolate ganache onto the other half. Twist on the tops.

Peanut butter & jam

1 (16-ounce) jar creamy peanut butter

1 (10-ounce) jar raspberry jam (purchased or recipe on page 95)

Fill a pastry bag with the peanut butter and pipe it onto half of each macaron bottom. Spoon ½ teaspoon of raspberry jam onto the other half, then twist on the tops.

CHAPTER 3

Fun Macaron Designs

Macarons make a great addition to any festive occasion. Match the colors of the shells to the event—pink or light blue for a baby shower, or red and green at Christmastime. Sprinkle on red, white, and blue stars to celebrate the Fourth of July, or candy leaves and tiny pumpkins for Halloween. Add sparkle with colored sugar or luster dust. Everything you'll need for the following special effects can be found at stores specializing in baking supplies, or online.

Macaron lollipops

These "lollipops" will delight children and grown-ups alike. This fun and fanciful way to present macarons is equally suitable for birthday parties, wedding buffets, or teatime at home.

WHAT YOU NEED:

macaron shells and filling

lollipop sticks

clear cellophane bags

ribbon

"contour round" Styrofoam cake dummy, covered with gold foil or other fancy paper

You can make your macaron lollipops in either of these two ways:

Insert the lollipop sticks before baking.

After piping the macarons, insert sticks into half of them (leave more space than usual between macarons). Bake and let cool completely, then join by pairs (one shell with a lollipop stick, one without) and fill with ganache or buttercream. Place them on a tray and cover them with plastic film. Let them rest a couple of hours in the refrigerator.

Insert the lollipop sticks after baking.

Fill pairs of baked macaron shells with ganache or buttercream and insert a stick into the filling of each pair.

Once assembled, place the lollipops on a tray, cover with plastic wrap, and refrigerate for a couple of hours. Once the filling has set, wrap them individually in clear cellophane bags and tie with ribbon. Poke the sticks into the Styrofoam base, and you have a lollipop bouquet for your buffet table.

***

Tower of macarons

You may have seen macaron "towers" featured in magazines and on websites as the latest thing in centerpieces. Now you can create your own tower of macarons for a party, a special dinner, or a wedding celebration. Impress your guests with several cones in different colors, or showcase a single big cone put together with rows of macarons in contrasting colors.

WHAT YOU NEED:

filled macarons

Styrofoam cone (select one with a wide base for stability), covered with gold foil or other fancy paper

toothpicks

Starting at the bottom edge of the Styrofoam cone, stab in a toothpick at a 45-degree angle, leaving a third of it sticking out; attach your first macaron as shown on the facing page. (Make sure the toothpick doesn't show through.) Continue around the cone, inserting toothpicks and attaching macarons. Repeat row by row until the cone is completely covered with macarons.

For a nice visual effect, you can work by rows of colors, or you can mix colors and flavors randomly. For the last macaron on the top of the cone, stab a toothpick in vertically and anchor the macaron in place. Beautiful!

✳ ✳ ✳

Sugar decorations for macarons

Sugar decorations that you make yourself—in the shape of flowers, stars, or anything else—can give a unique personal touch to your macarons. All the special supplies you'll need to create them can be purchased at a baking supply store or online.

WHAT YOU NEED:

fondant or gum paste (white)

powdered sugar

food coloring

modeling tools

small rolling pin

silicone mat or other smooth work surface

luster dust (gold, silver, copper, sparkle white, dust blue, pink…)

small brush (such as a new makeup brush or paintbrush)

cutters—butterfly, heart, daisy, seasonal, or any shapes you like

Soften a small amount of fondant or gum paste by working it in your hands. It needs to be soft and pliable but not sticky. If it sticks to your fingers, sprinkle on a little powdered sugar. To make colored shapes, add a few drops of food coloring while you're working the material in your hands. The result will be a nice marbled effect. For bright colors, add more food coloring, or you can buy fondant that's already colored.

Using your small rolling pin, roll out your fondant or gum paste on your work surface to a thickness of about ⅛ inch, then use your cutters or a knife to cut out shapes. Let your shapes dry, uncovered, until they harden, about 30 minutes. Then brush on some sparkling luster dust to give them a nice shiny effect.

To fasten your sugar creations to your macarons, dip a small brush into egg whites and apply where you want decorations to be, then stick them in place.

Wrap any leftover fondant airtight to use another time; it doesn't need to be refrigerated.

✳✳✳

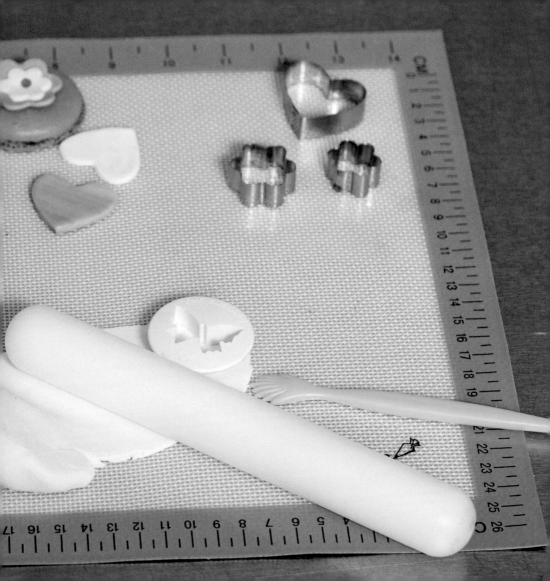

Appendix

APPENDIX

Bonus recipe: using leftover yolks

Crème brûlée

Makes 5 servings

This classic French dessert will help you use the egg yolks that remain after you make macaron shells. You'll need 5 shallow ramekins (each about 5½ inches in diameter) and—to create the burnt sugar crust—a kitchen torch. Serve with leftover macaron shells.

1 vanilla bean OR 1 teaspoon vanilla paste

1 cup whole milk

1 cup heavy cream

5 egg yolks

⅔ cup (4.2 ounces/120 grams) superfine granulated sugar

5 teaspoons raw sugar

Preheat oven to 230°F. If you're using a vanilla bean, split it in half lengthwise and scrape out the seeds. Drop the vanilla seeds or paste into a saucepan containing the milk. Begin heating over medium temperature. Meanwhile, beat together the yolks and the granulated sugar until smooth.

When the milk begins to boil, remove it from the heat and stir in the cold heavy cream, mixing well. Pour over the yolks and beat together quickly (you don't want the heat of the milk to cook the yolks). Pour the mixture through a strainer and distribute equally among 5 ramekins.

Bake at 230°F (255°F for a non-convection oven) for 50 to 60 minutes, or until the crème brûlée starts to turn dark yellow. Remove from the oven and let cool, then cover with plastic wrap and refrigerate for 6 hours (or up to 3 days). Thirty minutes before serving, remove from the refrigerator, take off the plastic wrap, and spread one 1 teaspoon raw sugar in each ramekin. Use your kitchen torch to turn the sugar into hot caramel crusts.

✺ CONVERSIONS

Measure	Equivalent	Metric
1 teaspoon	--	5 milliliters
1 tablespoon	3 teaspoons	15 milliliters
1 cup	16 tablespoons	250 milliliters
1 pint	2 cups	500 milliliters
1 quart	4 cups	1 liter
1 liter	4 cups + 3½ tablespoons	1000 milliliters
1 ounce (dry)	--	30 grams
1 pound	16 ounces	450 grams
2.21 pounds	35¼ ounces	1 kilogram

OTHER ULYSSES PRESS BOOKS

The Petit Four Cookbook: Adorably Delicious, Bite-Size Confections from the Dragonfly Cakes Bakery
Brooks Coulson Nguyen, $19.95

Delicate layers of moist cake, buttercream and marzipan, coated in decadent chocolate, petits fours are the quintessential bite-size indulgence. With step-by-step recipes and mouth-watering photos, *The Petit Four Cookbook* teaches you how to make these decorative French delights perfect for any occasion.

Sugar-Free Gluten-Free Baking and Desserts: Recipes for Healthy and Delicious Cookies, Cakes, Muffins, Scones, Pies, Puddings, Breads and Pizzas
Kelly Keough, $15.95

Shows readers how to bring taboo treats back to the baking sheet with savory recipes that swap wheat for wholesome alternatives like quinoa, arrowroot and tapioca starch, and trade in sugar for natural sweeteners like agave, yacon and stevia.

The I Love Trader Joe's Cookbook: Over 150 Delicious Recipes Using Only Foods from the World's Greatest Grocery Store *10th Anniversary Edition*

Cherie Mercer Twohy, **$19.95**

Based on the author's wildly popular, standing-room-only workshops, *The I Love Trader Joe's Cookbook* presents her top recipes for everything from crowd-pleasing hors d'oeuvres and tasty quick meals to gourmet entrées and world-class desserts.

The I Love Trader Joe's Party Cookbook: Delicious Recipes and Entertaining Ideas Using Only Foods and Drinks from the World's Greatest Grocery Store

Cherie Mercer Twohy, **$17.95**

With menus and plans for more than 25 celebrations, this indispensable entertaining guide is packed with mouth-watering recipes, do-ahead tips, and drink suggestions.

To order these books call 800-377-2542 or 510-601-8301, fax 510-601-8307, e-mail ulysses@ulyssespress.com, or write to Ulysses Press, P.O. Box 3440, Berkeley, CA 94703. All retail orders are shipped free of charge. California residents must include sales tax. Allow two to three weeks for delivery.